THE SINGING

CAERPHILLY
COUNTY BOROUGH COUNCIL
CYNGOR BWRDEISTREF SIROL
CAERFFILI

Please return / renew this item by the last date shown above
Dychwelwch / Adnewyddwch erbyn y dyddiad olaf y nodir yma

OXFORD
UNIVERSITY PRESS

Great Clarendon Street, Oxford, OX2 6DP,
United Kingdom

Oxford University Press is a department of the University of Oxford.
It furthers the University's objective of excellence in research, scholarship,
and education by publishing worldwide. Oxford is a registered trade mark of
Oxford University Press in the UK and in certain other countries

British Library Cataloguing in Publication Data
Data available

978-0-19-837756-6

1 3 5 7 9 10 8 6 4 2

Paper used in the production of this book is a natural, recyclable product
made from wood grown in sustainable forests. The manufacturing process
conforms to the environmental regulations of the country of origin.

Printed in China by Leo Paper Products Ltd.

Acknowledgements
Inside cover notes written by Becca Heddle
Author photograph by Maddie Joinson

Contents

Chapter 1
A Mysterious Song

Come close and I will tell you a story.
Every word of this story is true.

It all happened many years ago. It
happened in a place so far away that it
would take your feet many, many weeks
to carry you there.

In this faraway land, there was a man called Marka. He was a greedy and lazy man. He dreamed of having servants to do his work. He wanted someone to cook for him. He wanted someone to tie up his shoes for him. He even wanted someone to wash his face for him!

One day, Marka was walking through the long grass of a meadow. He was daydreaming of having servants who would cook for him and tie his shoes. "If only I could find a way to make my fortune!" he said to himself. "I could have servants to do everything for me!"

You see how lazy he was? If he was the sun, we would all be living in darkness because he would be too lazy to shine.

As he walked, he heard singing. It was singing so beautiful that he was forced to stop walking so that he could listen. It was singing that made a shiver travel down his back. It was singing that made him shake his head in wonder. He had to find the singer.

Marka searched and searched in the long grass. At last, he found the creature who was making the wonderful music – a tortoise!

"How can something so slow and heavy make such a beautiful sound?" he said.

"My shell is heavy but my voice is light," the tortoise told him.

Marka begged the tortoise to sing for him again. He crouched down beside her. As she sang, he thought that he had never heard such lovely music in all his life.

"Let me take you home with me," he said to the tortoise. "I must hear you sing every day."

"But I do not want to leave," the tortoise said. "I love my home. I can listen to the reeds whispering, and to the river rushing, and to the leaves rustling in the trees. The sounds around me help me sing."

Marka frowned. More than anything, he wanted to hear the tortoise sing again. Not only that – he wanted to take her home with him so he could hear her sing every day. He didn't care that the tortoise loved her home. All he wanted was to find a way to take her to *his* home.

You remember how I told you earlier that he was a greedy and lazy man? Well, now you can see he was greedy, lazy *and* selfish. If he had a bowl of fruit he would not give you even a single piece of it – not even a rotten banana!

Chapter 2
Marka's Lies

"Please come with me," Marka pleaded.
"I will treat you well. I will give you a
bed of the softest sheets and a bowl of the
purest water."

The tortoise laughed. "The river reeds
make the softest bed, and the river water is
the most refreshing I could ever taste."

Marka pleaded with the tortoise.
"Please will you come, just for a short visit?
I promise to bring you back when you are
ready to go home."

Well, reader, I hope you are ready to
hiss and boo! For Marka did not intend
to bring the tortoise back at all! He had
decided to say anything and promise
everything to persuade the tortoise to
come with him.

The tortoise sighed. "I will come with you if you will promise me one thing."

"Anything!" Marka cried. "Everything!" (We know that he was lying, don't we?)

"You must not tell anyone about my singing," the tortoise said.

"I promise," Marka said. The promise slipped from his lips as easily as water slipping over pebbles.

"Then carry me carefully and when we arrive at your house, I will sing again, just for you."

Marka clapped his hands. "I will care for you well," he told the tortoise. Quickly, he carried the tortoise off to his home before she could change her mind.

At first, all was well. Marka brought
the tortoise everything she needed and in
return she filled his little house with song.

Every time the tortoise sang, Marka
was struck again at how beautiful the
music was. "It is like the sun is sitting in
my house," he said to himself.

Marka was happy but the tortoise was
not. "I miss the sound of the wind in the
reeds, and the sound of the river running
over the pebbles in the river bed," she said.
"When will you take me home?"

"Soon," Marka told her. "For now, sing again. Sing of the wind in the reeds and of the river running over the stones, and you won't miss them any more."

The tortoise sang about everything she missed, but it only made her miss her home more.

And so it continued. Every morning, the tortoise asked when Marka would take her back again. And every morning, Marka lied and said, "Soon." But really, he had decided to keep her forever!

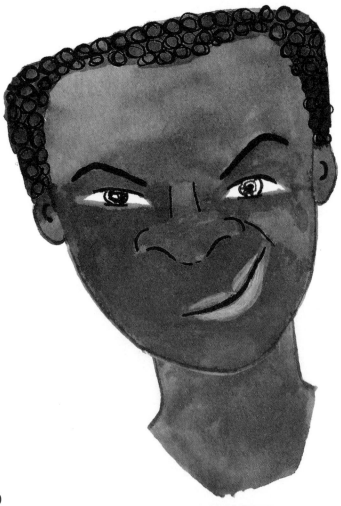

Chapter 3
Marka Makes a Plan

One day, as Marka went into town to do some shopping, he looked at the people around him. He thought of how much they would admire the tortoise's singing if they could hear it. Perhaps they would even *pay* to hear it.

"And if they would pay me, then I could become rich," he thought. "And if I became rich, then I could have servants to cook for me and tie my shoes. I could have servants for everything!"

He pictured himself surrounded by servants: one offering him a cool drink in a tall glass, another a plate of fresh fruit, another holding out clothes of silk. He walked on, daydreaming.

"I would be the envy of the town!" thought Marka. "People would turn and whisper to each other, 'There goes Marka, the man who has that miracle of creatures, the singing tortoise!'"

You see, reader, Marka had forgotten
his promise to tell no one about the
tortoise. To Marka, a promise was
something you made to get what you
want, not something you had to keep.

So Marka began boasting about his tortoise. As he was buying some fruit at the market, a woman nearby was singing. When some people complimented her on her pretty voice, he broke in. "If you think she's got a nice voice, you should hear my tortoise. She has the most beautiful voice in the world!"

"A singing tortoise?" the fruit seller laughed. "This I have to see!"

Everyone at the market crowded around Marka asking questions. "How can a tortoise sing?" "How did you find her?" And over and over again, "When can we hear her?"

Marka was delighted – his plan was working! He frowned and shook his head. "I don't know if she will want to sing for anyone but me," he said.

Of course, Marka knew perfectly well that the tortoise *didn't* want to sing for anyone else. But he said this because he thought it would make the people want to hear the tortoise even more.

Many people became excited. "Please let us hear her," they told him. "We will give you gold if she is as good as you say."

The fruit seller laughed again. "I don't think this tortoise of yours sings at all."

"Well, come and hear her then," said Marka. "You'll see that my tortoise sings better than anyone you have heard."

"And better than any other tortoise," said the fruit seller. "Because tortoises can't sing!"

Marka announced that anyone who wanted to hear his tortoise should come the next morning. He went home thinking about how many people might come to his house and pay him gold.

"Perhaps it won't be many," he thought, "but if they hear my tortoise sing, they will tell others and then they will pay, too. Soon I will be rich and everyone in the town will talk of me!" He didn't think about his promise to the tortoise. He was sure that once everyone had praised her singing, she would be happy.

"Everyone likes to be told they are good at something. Everyone likes to be told they are wonderful. Everyone likes to make lots of money," he said to himself.

You see, because Marka was greedy and vain, he thought everyone must be like him. But we know that (luckily) not everyone is!

Chapter 4
A Surprise

Marka rose early the next day. Although usually he was lazy and liked to lie in bed until the last possible moment, that morning he rose out of bed at first light. He was thinking of how the people in the town would look at him when they had heard the tortoise sing.

"Maybe I will take the tortoise to other places, too," he thought.

"We can go from village to village and town to town and city to city. I will become so famous that I won't have to pay for my clothes or food." Marka prepared his morning meal and took some fresh grass to the tortoise. "I hope you are ready to sing your sweetest song today," he told the tortoise.

"I will sing as I always do and always
have," the tortoise said. "Why should I
sing more sweetly today?"

Marka tapped his nose and smiled.
"It's a surprise!"

The tortoise sighed. "The surprise I
would like is to be taken home," she said.

"Soon, soon," Marka said. "I will take
you home soon."

The tortoise sighed again. She had realized by now that Marka did not tell the truth. Marka's promises had the same weight as clouds – no weight at all. The tortoise watched Marka as he put on his finest clothes and tidied up his house. She could see that he was up to something but she did not know what.

There was a knock on the door.

"Oh!" Marka said, pretending to be surprised. "A visitor!" He opened the door and then gasped. Standing on the step was the fruit seller, and behind him stretched a long, long line of people from the town.

The line wound down the street and
around the corner like a snake of many
colours.

"Oh!" said Marka again – this time
he really *was* surprised!

More people than he had ever imagined had come to hear his tortoise. Marka grinned – all his dreams were about to come true!

Chapter 5
Marka Gets into Trouble

"Well, let's hear your singing tortoise
then," said the fruit seller with a big grin
on his face. "If she can sing as well as you
say, I'll give you free fruit for the rest of
your life. And if she can sing at all, I'll
give you free fruit for the week."

The fruit seller laughed and some people behind him laughed, too. Others pressed forward, all eager to see and hear the singing tortoise.

"You will need to pay me if you wish to hear the tortoise," Marka said, with a look of cunning.

"We will pay you *after* we hear the tortoise sing," the fruit seller told him and he pushed past Marka and went into the house. Marka frowned but he stepped aside to let the others come in.

Soon Marka's house was full of people.
People settled on Marka's chairs. Mothers
and fathers held their children on their
laps or put them on their shoulders so that
they could see. A grandmother perched on
a stool and other people clambered on to
a table and any other surface they could
find. The house was so crowded that no
one could move.

"Where is the tortoise?" The fruit seller shouted from the corner of the room.

"Yes, where is the tortoise?" called a few others, who were becoming uncomfortable as yet more people crammed into the house. "Let's hear her sing!"

Marka squeezed and wormed his way across the room and into the bedroom where the tortoise sat.

"What a surprise!" he told her. "All these people have come to hear you sing."

"You promised you would not tell," the
tortoise said. She looked at him sadly.

"It is not right to keep a talent like
yours a secret," Marka said. "Think of the
riches we will have when people hear your
beautiful voice. All the gold in the world
will be ours for the asking."

"I do not want all the gold in the
world," the tortoise said. "I want only my
home in the wild. I want to hear the wind
in the reeds and the water running over the
pebbles in the river bed."

"If you sing," Marka told her.
"Everyone will praise you."

"I do not want to be praised," the tortoise said. "I want only to sit quietly by the river bed and praise the wonder of what is around me."

Marka picked up the tortoise. "If you will sing for all these people now," he said, "I promise I will take you home after they have gone."

The tortoise looked at him. "You made a promise to me before and you did not keep it," she said.

Marka smiled. "I promise I will keep this one."

(Do you believe Marka intended to keep his promise? No, neither do I.)

The tortoise said nothing as Marka carried her through to the next room. Excited chattering broke out as Marka entered and everyone saw the tortoise: "Is that her?" "When is she going to start?"

Chapter 6
Marka Learns a Lesson

Marka held the tortoise up high. "Here she is!" he cried. "A marvel of nature! The most amazing creature in the world! A singer of such beauty you will laugh, you will cry, you will shout with wonder!"

"We're going to shout with impatience if she doesn't start!" called the fruit seller.

Marka smiled and brought the tortoise close. "It is time to sing now," he whispered.

The tortoise looked at him, her eyes full of sadness, but she did not sing.

Marka smiled again, a little nervously. "Sing, my beauty," he told her. "Everyone is waiting."

The tortoise did not even shake her head. She stayed perfectly still – and perfectly silent.

"That's a very quiet song she's singing," the fruit seller said. "Tell her to sing up a little, will you?"

Marka frowned. "You must sing now," he said to the tortoise. "Sing!"

Still the tortoise remained silent.

The fruit seller began to laugh. "Just as I thought – not a note. He's just been trying to get our money."

"SING!" Marka shouted at the tortoise.

"That's not right," said the fruit seller. "I don't like the way you are treating her – or us."

The crowd grew angry. They had come
to hear the tortoise sing and all they could
see was a perfectly ordinary, silent tortoise.

"He's a trickster!" cried an old woman.
"Trying to get our money for nothing!"

"He's a liar!" shouted others.

Marka looked around at all the angry,
disappointed faces, and realized that he
was in trouble …

The fruit seller made his way over to
Marka. "Why is this tortoise locked up in
your house? Shouldn't she be living out in
the open?"

The tortoise looked up at Marka, her
eyes wide and sad.

Marka thought of the reeds by the river.
He thought of the water chuckling over
the pebbles. He thought of the wind as it
tickled the grass where the tortoise slept.
He looked around at his small house where
no wind blew and no river ran.

He felt something in his heart stir. "I'm sorry," Marka told the tortoise. He looked up at the crowd of people. "I'm sorry," he told them.

"You should be!" said the grandmother who had been sitting on a stool. "I was going to see my daughter, but I came to hear your tortoise instead. I have wasted my whole morning."

Chapter 7
Marka Becomes Honest

The crowd grumbled as they left, complaining that Marka had wasted their time and tried to trick them out of their money.

The fruit seller was the last to leave. "It will be a long time before anyone in the town will trust you again," he said to Marka.

Marka was ashamed. "I have been foolish, dreaming of riches instead of working for them. I have lied when I should have told the truth, and broken my promises."

"Then you must try and win everyone's trust back," the fruit seller told him.

Marka nodded. "Yes. But first I must return this tortoise to her home as I promised her. Then … well, then I must try and think how to find work when nobody trusts me."

The fruit seller looked at him. "Are you really, truly sorry?"

"Yes," Marka said. "I am." He felt lighter as he realized he was telling the truth.

The fruit seller smiled. "Well then, come along to my stall at first light tomorrow morning and I will give you work."

Marka's mouth dropped open. "You will?"

The fruit seller laughed. "Everyone deserves a second chance." He clapped Marka on the shoulder. "Besides, a singing tortoise! What a good story that was!" He waved as he left. "See you at first light tomorrow!"

When the fruit seller had left, Marka turned to the tortoise. "Now it is time for me to keep my promise."

Marka took the tortoise back to the place he had found her. He placed her gently on the ground near to the river where the water rushed over the pebbles, where the wind whispered in the reeds and where the leaves rustled in the trees.

"There," Marka said. "You are home at last. I am sorry I lied to you."

"Thank you," said the tortoise. "I am glad to be home."

Marka smiled. "If you will let me, I will come and visit you sometimes, but I will never take you away from where you belong again."

"If you promise that – and keep your promise," the tortoise said, "then every time you come I will sing to you."

59

And this is how it was, reader. From
that day, Marka worked hard for the fruit
seller, carrying the heavy boxes of fruit
from the fruit seller's cart to the stall.

Once he discovered how good it felt to
work hard and earn his own money, he
forgot his dreams about servants. In time,
the people of the town forgot Marka's story
and he became known as the most honest
man in the town.

The fruit seller teased Marka about the 'singing tortoise' every now and then but Marka only smiled. Finally, even the fruit seller forgot about the morning when the tortoise lay silent in Marka's hands.

But every week, Marka went to the place where the reeds whispered in the wind and the river ran. He sat and listened to the beautiful song of the tortoise as she sang of the wonders of the world around her. As Marka listened to her beautiful song, he knew he was truly rich at last.

About the author

I like writing all kinds of stories. *The Singing Tortoise* is a folk tale – a story that has been told for so many years that no one can remember who first told it. I like the way folk tales can change each time they are told, with different people adding different details. One of the changes I made was to add the fruit seller to the story. I like him because although he laughs at Marka, he is kind in the end and gives him another chance. Everyone deserves a second chance! And that's why I also gave Marka a happier ending!